African Principles on the Law Applicable to International Commercial Contracts

Jan L Neels

Professor of Private International Law

University of Johannesburg

UJ Press

African Principles on the Law Applicable to International Commercial Contracts

Published by UJ Press
University of Johannesburg
Library
Auckland Park Kingsway Campus
PO Box 524
Auckland Park
2006
https://ujonlinepress.uj.ac.za/

First published 2023

https://doi.org/10.36615/9781776447411

978-1-7764474-0-4 (Paperback)
978-1-7764474-1-1 (PDF)
978-1-7764474-2-8 (EPUB)
978-1-7764474-3-5 (XML)

Cover design: Hester Roets, UJ Graphic Design Studio
Typeset in 10/13pt Merriweather Light

Contents

SDG

"Africa is today at mid-course, in transition from the Africa of Yesterday to the Africa of Tomorrow. Even as we stand here, we move from the past into the future. The task on which we have embarked, the making of Africa, will not wait. We must act, to shape and mould the future and leave our imprint on events as they slip past into history" (Emperor Haile Selassie *"1963 Address to African Leaders (25 May 1963)"* in D P Curtin (ed) **Speeches of the Emperor Haile Selassie** *(Dalcassian, Philadelphia, 2018)* 77).

Introduction

The formulation of the African Principles on the Law Applicable to International Commercial Contracts[1] is a project of the Research Centre for Private International Law in Emerging Countries at the University of Johannesburg. The African Principles, which instrument sets forth general principles for determining the law applicable to international commercial contracts,[2] are envisaged to become a regional model law, or even a binding regional convention, for the Member States of the African Union.[3] They could also be considered by regional economic integration and similar organisations, for instance

---

1   Jan L Neels "The African Principles on the Law Applicable to International Commercial Contracts – a first drafting experiment" 2020 *Uniform Law Review/Revue de droit uniforme* 426. See for discussions of the project: Jan L Neels "International commercial law emerging in Africa" 2022 *Potchefstroom Electronic Law Journal* (Special Edition: *Festschrift Charl Hugo*) DOI http://dx.doi.org/10.17159/1727-3781/2022/v25i0a14381; Jan L Neels and Eesa A Fredericks "An introduction to the African Principles of Commercial Private International Law" 2018 *Stellenbosch Law Review* 347; and Jan L Neels and Eesa A Fredericks "The African Principles of Commercial Private International Law and the Hague Principles" in Daniel Girsberger, Thomas Kadner Graziano and Jan L Neels (gen eds) *Choice of Law in International Commercial Contracts. Global Perspectives on the Hague Principles* (Oxford University Press, 2021) 239. The following two chapters are to be published during 2023: Jan L Neels "The Southern African Development Community and the African Principles on the Law Applicable to International Commercial Contracts"; and Jan L Neels, Eesa A Fredericks and Solomon Okorley "UNIDROIT and Africa – UNIDROIT Principles and African Principles".

2   See Preamble par 1. Also see Art 1(1)–(2).

3   See Preamble par 2. See www.au.int.

EAC,[4] ECOWAS,[5] OHADA[6] and SADC,[7] or by national legislators on the African continent.[8] In addition, they may be used by African courts in the interpretation, supplementation and development of the rules of private international law of contract,[9] and also by arbitral tribunals, whenever appropriate and whether the tribunal is seated in Africa or elsewhere.[10]

The existence of a reliable transnational legal infrastructure in respect of international commercial law, including commercial private international law, is a prerequisite for investor confidence, inclusive economic growth, sustainable development, and the ultimate alleviation of poverty on the African continent. The proposed African Principles may contribute to sustainable growth on a long-term basis. They are essential to the further development of the African Continental Free Trade Area, which was established in 2018.[11]

The first experiment in the drafting of the African Principles on the Law Applicable to International Commercial Contracts was published in the 2020 *Uniform Law Review/Revue de droit uniforme*,[12] which is edited by UNIDROIT and published by Oxford University Press. The proposed instrument is again made available in this booklet,[13] together with translations in

---

4   East African Community. See www.eac.int.

5   Economic Community of West African States. See www.ecowas.int.

6   *Organisation pour l'harmonisation en Afrique du droit des affaires* (Organisation for the Harmonisation of Business Law in Africa). See www.ohada.org.

7   Southern African Development Community. See www.sadc.int.

8   See Preamble par 2.

9   See Preamble par 3.

10   See Preamble par 4.

11   For information on AfCFTA, see www.tralac.org.

12   Neels (n 1, 2020).

13   Changes were made to Art 4(1)(d) (various suggestions), Art 6(1)(f) (Prof Fekadu P Gebremeskel, University of Addis Ababa), Art 8 (Prof Sieg (G T S) Eiselen, University of South Africa), Art 15(1) (Prof Chukwuma S A Okoli, University of Birmingham, and Prof Richard F Oppong, California

French (by Dr Justin Monsenepwo) and Portuguese (by Prof Rui Dias and Ms Rita Duarte).

The Hague Principles on Choice of Law in International Commercial Contracts[14] and the Rome I Regulation on the Law Applicable to Contractual Obligations[15] were utilised as the primary models for the African Principles on the Law Applicable to International Commercial Contracts. The following conflicts, procedural and substantive instruments also played a role: the Rome Convention on the Law Applicable to Contractual Obligations;[16] the Mexico City Convention on the Law Applicable to International Contracts;[17] the Rome II Regulation on the Law Applicable to Non-Contractual Obligations;[18] the Hague Convention on Choice of Court Agreements;[19] the Hague Convention on the Recognition and Enforcement of Foreign Judgments in Civil or Commercial Matters;[20] the UNCITRAL Model Law on International Commercial Arbitration;[21] the UNIDROIT Principles on International Commercial Contracts;[22] and the United Nations Convention on the International Sale of Goods.[23] A limited number of further sources were considered, including preliminary draft legislation on the law applicable to contractual obligations intended for the Democratic Republic

---

Western School of Law) and Art 17. The proposals were primarily made during the Pan-African Conference on the African Principles on the Law Applicable to International Commercial Contracts, 31 May and 1-2 June 2023, University of Johannesburg. Many other recommendations were made, and they will be considered for the purposes of a possible next edition of the African Principles.

14   (2015) (Hague Principles).
15   (2008) (Rome I Regulation).
16   (1980) (Rome Convention).
17   Inter-American Convention on the Law Applicable to International Contracts (CIDIP-V) (1994) (Mexico City Convention).
18   (2007) (Rome II Regulation).
19   (2005).
20   (2019).
21   (1985/2006).
22   (2016) (UPICC).
23   (1980) (CISG).

of the Congo, as proposed by a working group facilitated by the Research Centre for Private International Law in Emerging Countries (University of Johannesburg) at its meeting in October 2019.[24]

The author would like to thank the consecutive deans of the Faculty of Law at the University of Johannesburg for their personal and financial support of the project: Prof Derek van der Merwe (later Pro-Vice-Chancellor and Deputy Vice-Chancellor), Prof George N Barrie, Prof Jannie M Otto, Prof Patrick H O'Brien (later General Counsel), Prof Letlhokwa G Mpedi (later Deputy Vice-Chancellor and, currently, Vice-Chancellor) and Prof Wesahl Domingo. He would also like to express his gratitude towards Prof Bettine Jansen van Vuuren (then Senior Director: Strategic Initiatives and Administration, currently Registrar), the translators into French and Portuguese (mentioned above), Dr Craig MacKenzie (linguistic revision: English version), Mr Wikus van Zyl (Manager: UJ Press), Ms Hester Roets (UJ Graphic Design Studio), and the following (former) staff members of the South African Department of International Relations and Cooperation: Adv Sandea de Wet, Dr Theunis Kotze, Mr Andre Smit, Adv André Stemmet, Mr Siya Mpongosha, Ms Ellouise King and Adv Keke (M A) Motsepe.

Stakeholders and other interested parties are requested to send any proposals for the improvement of the Principles to Prof Jan L Neels at jlneels@uj.ac.za and africanprinciples@gmail.com. Please also inform us of the use of the African Principles in legislation, case law and academic work.

---

24   See Justin Monsenepwo "L'Avant-projet de Loi sur la loi applicable aux obligations contractuelles en droit international privé congolais" in T K Bala *et al Adoption des mineurs et migrations en droit interne, international et comparé* Tome II *Mélanges en l'honneur du Professeur Paolo Morozzo della Rocca* (Editions Universitaires Européennes, Paris, 2021) 604.

Abbreviations

AfCFTA	African Continental Free Trade Area
African Principles	African Principles on the Law Applicable to International Commercial Contracts
CISG	United Nations Convention on the International Sale of Goods (1980)
DRC draft	Preliminary draft legislation on the law applicable to contractual obligations intended for the Democratic Republic of the Congo (working group, RCPILEC, 2019)
Hague Convention on Choice of Court Agreements	Convention on Choice of Court Agreements (2005)
Hague Convention on the Recognition and Enforcement of Foreign Judgments in Civil or Commercial Matters	Convention on the Recognition and Enforcement of Foreign Judgments in Civil or Commercial Matters (2019)
Hague Principles	Principles on Choice of Law in International Commercial Contracts (2015)
HCCH Principles	Principles on Choice of Law in International Commercial Contracts (2015)
Mexico City Convention	Inter-American Convention on the Law Applicable to International Contracts (1994)
OHADA	*Organisation pour l'harmonisation en Afrique du droit des affaires*

RCPILEC	Research Centre for Private International Law in Emerging Countries, University of Johannesburg
Rome I Regulation	Rome I Regulation on the Law Applicable to Contractual Obligations (2008)
Rome II Regulation	Rome II Regulation on the Law Applicable to Non-Contractual Obligations (2007)
Rome Convention	Rome Convention on the Law Applicable to Contractual Obligations (1980)
UNCITRAL Model Law on International Commercial Arbitration	UNCITRAL Model Law on International Commercial Arbitration (1985/2006)
UPICC	UNIDROIT Principles on International Commercial Contracts (2016)

African Principles on the Law Applicable to International Commercial Contracts

Preamble

1   This instrument sets forth general principles for determining the law applicable to international commercial contracts.

2   They may be used as a model for national, regional and supranational legislative instruments in Africa.

3   They may be used by African courts in the interpretation, supplementation and development of the rules of private international law of contract.

4   They may be used by arbitral tribunals in the interpretation, supplementation and development of the rules of private international law of contract, whenever appropriate and whether the tribunal is seated in Africa or elsewhere.

Article 1
Scope of the Principles

1   These Principles apply, in situations involving a conflict of laws, to international contractual obligations in civil and commercial matters, where each party is acting in the exercise of its trade or profession.

2   These Principles do not address the law governing the following types of contracts –

    (a)   consumer contracts;
    (b)   contracts of carriage;
    (c)   employment contracts;
    (d)   insurance contracts.

3   These Principles do not address the law governing arbitration agreements and agreements on choice of court.

4   These Principles do not address the law governing the following topics –

(a)   the capacity of natural persons;
(b)   companies or other collective bodies and trusts;
(c)   evidence and procedure;
(d)   insolvency;
(e)   the issue of whether an agent is able to bind a principal to a third party;
(f)   negotiable instruments;
(g)   the proprietary effects of contracts;
(h)   revenue, customs or administrative matters.

Article 2
Universal application

Any law specified by this instrument is applicable whether or not it is the law of a Member State of the African Union.

Article 3
Freedom of choice of law

1   A contract is governed by the law chosen by the parties.
2   The parties may choose –

(a)   the law applicable to the whole contract or to one or more aspects or parts thereof; and
(b)   different laws for different aspects or parts of the contract.

3   No connection is required between the law chosen and the parties or their transaction.
4   The choice may be made or modified at any time. A choice or modification made after the contract has been concluded does not prejudice its formal validity or the rights of third parties.

5   A choice of law cannot be contested solely on the ground that the contract to which it applies is not valid.

Article 4
Choice of rules of law; incorporation by reference

1   A choice of one or more of the following instruments is recognised on the same level as the choice of the law of a country:

    (a) the UNIDROIT Principles of International Commercial Contracts;

    (b) a treaty, as defined in the United Nations Convention on the Law of Treaties;

    (c) the Uniform Customs and Practice for Documentary Credits;

    (d) any instrument issued under the auspices of a regional economic integration organisation or an international, supranational or regional intergovernmental organisation, including any instrument issued by the *Organisation pour l'harmonisation en Afrique du droit des affaires.*

2   If the parties choose an instrument in terms of paragraph (1)(b), (c) or (d), the UNIDROIT Principles of International Commercial Contracts may be used in its interpretation and supplementation.

3   If the parties choose the general principles of law, the *lex mercatoria*, international commercial law or the like to govern their contract, the following instruments may be applied, where relevant –

    (a) the UNIDROIT Principles of International Commercial Contracts;

    (b) the United Nations Convention on the International Sale of Goods, as interpreted and supplemented by the UNIDROIT Principles of International Commercial Contracts;

    (c) the Uniform Customs and Practice for Documentary Credits.

4   The law applicable to the contract in terms of this instrument determines whether the parties may incorporate by reference any set of rules or standard terms not listed in paragraph (1).

Article 5
Express and tacit choice of law

1   A choice of law, or any modification of a choice of law, can be made expressly or tacitly.

2   A tacit choice of law must be manifestly clear from the provisions of the contract, the circumstances of the case, or both.

3   An agreement between the parties to confer jurisdiction on a court or an arbitral tribunal to determine disputes under the contract is not in itself equivalent to a choice of law.

4   An agreement between the parties to confer jurisdiction on a court or a localised arbitral tribunal may be taken into account in the determination of a tacit choice of law.

Article 6
Applicable law in the absence of choice of law

1   To the extent that the law applicable to the contract has not been chosen by the parties, the law governing the contract is to be determined as follows:

(a)   a contract for the sale of goods is governed by the law of the country of the habitual residence of the seller;

(b)   a contract for the provision of services is governed by the law of the country of the habitual residence of the service provider;

(c)   a contract relating to a right *in rem* in immovable property or to a tenancy of immovable property is governed by the law of the country where the property is situated;

(d) a franchise contract is governed by the law of the country of the habitual residence of the franchisee;

(e) a distribution contract is governed by the law of the country of the habitual residence of the distributor;

(f) a contract for the sale of goods by auction is governed by the law of the country where the auction takes place.

2 Where the contract is not covered by paragraph (1) or where the elements of the contract would be covered by more than one of points (a) to (f) of paragraph (1), the contract is governed by the law of the country of the habitual residence of the party required to effect the performance which is most characteristic of the contract.

3 Where it is clear from all the circumstances of the case that the contract is manifestly more closely connected with a country other than that indicated in paragraphs (1) or (2), the contract is governed by the law of that other country.

4 Where the law applicable cannot be determined pursuant to paragraphs 1 or 2, the contract is governed by the law of the country with which it is most closely connected.

Article 7
Role of international instruments

The law applicable to a contract by virtue of this instrument may be interpreted, supplemented and developed along the lines of the instruments listed in Article 4(3).

Article 8
Consent and material validity; choice of law in the battle of forms

1 The existence and material validity of a contract, or of any provision in a contract, must be determined by the law which would govern it under this instrument if the contract or provision were valid.

2   Nevertheless, the law of the habitual residence of a party determines whether that party has consented to the contract, or any provision in the contract, if, in the particular circumstances, it would be unreasonable to make that determination under the law specified in paragraph (1).

3   If the parties have used two sets of standard terms designating different laws, or if a law is designated in one of the sets of standard terms only, there is no express choice of law.

Article 9
Formal validity

1   A choice of law is not subject to any requirement as to form unless otherwise agreed by the parties.

2   Without prejudice to paragraph (1), a contract is formally valid if it complies with the requirements in this regard of at least one of the following legal systems:

   (a)   the law of the country of the conclusion of the contract, as determined according to (i) the law of the forum, or (ii) the law applicable to the contract by virtue of this instrument;

   (b)   the law applicable to the contract in terms of this instrument;

   (c)   the law of the country of the habitual residence of any one of the parties under the contract;

   (d)   the law of the country of the habitual residence of the agent of any one of the parties under the contract;

   (e)   the law of the country of the agreed place of any substantial performance under the contract.

3   As an exception to paragraph (2), but without prejudice to paragraph (1), the formal validity of a provision in a contract with the subject matter of a right *in rem* in immovable property, or of a tenancy of immovable property, is governed by the law of the country where the immovable is situated.

Article 10
Renvoi

The application of the law of any country specified by this instrument entails the application of the rules of law in force in that country other than its rules of private international law, unless the parties expressly provide otherwise.

Article 11
Overriding mandatory provisions

1   Overriding mandatory provisions are rules of law which are regarded as crucial by a country for safeguarding its public interests (including its political, social or economic organisation) to such an extent that they are applicable to any situation falling within their scope, irrespective of the law otherwise applicable to the contract under this instrument.

2   The overriding mandatory rules of the law governing the contract by virtue of this instrument are in principle applicable.

3   Effect may be given to the overriding mandatory rules of –

   (a)   the law of the forum;
   (b)   the law of the country of the agreed place of any substantial performance under the contract (including the country of commencement, continuation or completion of such performance).

4   In exceptional circumstances, the overriding mandatory rules of another country may be applied, provided that such law has a manifestly close connection to the particular situation.

5   In considering whether to give effect to any of the overriding mandatory rules mentioned in paragraph (3) or (4), regard must be had to their nature and purpose and to the consequences of their application or non-application.

Article 12
Public policy of the forum

The application of a provision of the law applicable in terms of this instrument may be refused only if such application would be manifestly incompatible with fundamental notions of the public policy of the forum.

Article 13
Scope of the law applicable to the contract

1   The law applicable to a contract by virtue of this instrument governs all aspects of the contract between the parties, including but not limited to –

   (a) interpretation;
   (b) rights and obligations arising from the contract;
   (c) the various ways of extinguishing obligations, and prescription and limitation periods;
   (d) the consequences of the formal or material invalidity of the contract;
   (e) burden of proof and legal presumptions;
   (f) pre-contractual obligations.

2

   (a) The law applicable to the contract by virtue of this instrument governs performance and the consequences of a total or partial breach of obligations, including the assessment of damages in as far as such is governed by rules of law.
   (b) However, a court or arbitral tribunal may refuse to award damages in terms of the law applicable by virtue of paragraph (a) to the extent that the damages would exceed compensation for actual loss (exemplary or punitive damages).
   (c) Nevertheless, a court or arbitral tribunal must take into account whether and to what extent exemplary or punitive damages in terms of the law applicable to the contract serve to cover costs and expenses relating to the procedure.

(d) In relation to the manner of performance and the steps to be taken in the event of defective performance, the law of the country of the agreed place of performance must be taken into account.

Article 14
Set-off

Set-off is governed by the law applicable to the claim against which the right to set-off is asserted, unless otherwise agreed by the parties.

Article 15
Habitual residence

1   For the purposes of this instrument, the habitual residence of companies and other bodies, corporate or unincorporated, is in the country of their central administration.

2   The habitual residence of a natural person acting in the course of his or her business activities is in the country of his or her principal place of business.

3   Where the contract is concluded in the course of the operations of a branch, agency or any other establishment, or if, under the contract, performance is the responsibility of such a branch, agency or establishment, the country where the branch, agency or any other establishment is located must be treated as the country of habitual residence.

4   For the purposes of determining habitual residence, the relevant point in time is the moment of the conclusion of the contract.

Article 16
Interpretation and uniformity of application

In the interpretation of this instrument, its regional character and international relevance, and the need to promote uniformity in its application must be taken into account.

Article 17
Entry into force and application in time

This instrument was adopted by the African Union on [date] and applies to contracts concluded as from [date]. In disputes relating to contracts concluded prior to this date, the court or arbitral tribunal may take the provisions of this instrument into account.

African Principles on the Law Applicable to International Commercial Contracts (with references)

This version contains references to corresponding provisions in international, supranational and regional instruments.

Preamble

1   This instrument sets forth general principles for determining the law applicable to international commercial contracts.[25]
2   They may be used as a model for national, regional and supranational legislative instruments in Africa.[26]
3   They may be used by African courts in the interpretation, supplementation and development of the rules of private international law of contract.[27]
4   They may be used by arbitral tribunals in the interpretation, supplementation and development of the rules of private international law of contract, whenever appropriate and whether the tribunal is seated in Africa or elsewhere.[28]

Article 1
Scope of the Principles

1   These Principles apply, in situations involving a conflict of laws, to international contractual obligations in civil

---

25   *Cf* Hague Principles, Preamble Par 1; UPICC, Preamble Par 1.
26   *Cf* Hague Principles, Preamble Par 2.
27   *Cf* Hague Principles, Preamble Par 3 and 4; UPICC, Preamble Par 5 and 6.
28   *Cf* Hague Principles, Preamble Par 3 and 4.

and commercial matters, where each party is acting in the exercise of its trade or profession.[29]

2 These Principles do not address the law governing the following types of contracts –

 (a) consumer contracts;[30]
 (b) contracts of carriage;[31]
 (c) employment contracts;[32]
 (d) insurance contracts.[33]

3 These Principles do not address the law governing arbitration agreements and agreements on choice of court.[34]

4 These Principles do not address the law governing the following topics –

 (a) the capacity of natural persons;[35]
 (b) companies or other collective bodies and trusts;[36]
 (c) evidence and procedure;[37]
 (d) insolvency;[38]

---

29 *Cf* Hague Principles, Art 1(1); Rome I Regulation, Art 1(1).

30 *Cf* Hague Principles, Art 1(1). See the specific arrangement in Art 6 of the Rome I Regulation.

31 See the specific arrangement in Art 5 of the Rome I Regulation.

32 See the specific arrangement in Art 8 of the Rome I Regulation.

33 See the specific arrangement in Art 7 of the Rome I Regulation.

34 *Cf* Hague Principles, Art 1(3)(b); Rome I Regulation, Art 1(2)(e).

35 *Cf* Hague Principles, Art 1(3)(a); Rome I Regulation, Art 1(2)(a). See Art 13 of the Rome I Regulation for a partial conflicts rule on the contractual capacity of a natural person. For an alternative proposal in this regard, see Eesa A Fredericks, *Contractual Capacity in Private International Law* (Meijers Research Institute, Leiden 2016) 248-249.

36 *Cf* Hague Principles, Art 1(3)(c); Rome I Regulation, Art 1(2)(f).

37 *Cf* Rome I Regulation, Art 1(3).

38 *Cf* Hague Principles, Art 1(3)(d); Rome I Regulation, Art 1(2)(f).

(e) the issue of whether an agent is able to bind a principal to a third party;[39]

(f) negotiable instruments;[40]

(g) the proprietary effects of contracts;[41]

(h) revenue, customs or administrative matters.[42]

Article 2
Universal application

Any law specified by this instrument is applicable whether or not it is the law of a Member State of the African Union.[43]

Article 3
Freedom of choice of law

1   A contract is governed by the law chosen by the parties.[44]

2   The parties may choose –

(a) the law applicable to the whole contract or to one or more aspects[45] or parts thereof;[46] and

(b) different laws for different aspects[47] or parts of the contract.[48]

---

39   *Cf* Hague Principles, Art 1(3)(f); Rome I Regulation, Art 1(2)(g).

40   *Cf* Rome I Regulation, Art 1(2)(d).

41   *Cf* Hague Principles, Art 1(3)(e).

42   *Cf* Rome I Regulation, Art 1(1).

43   *Cf* Rome I Regulation, Art 2.

44   Hague Principles, Art 2(1); *cf* Rome I Regulation, Art 3(1); UNCITRAL Model Law on International Commercial Arbitration, Art 28(1).

45   Hague Conference on Private International Law, *Principles on Choice of Law in International Commercial Contracts* (HCCH, The Hague 2015) (official commentary on the Hague Principles), illustration 2.2.

46   *Cf* Hague Principles, Art 2(2)(a); Rome I Regulation, Art 3(1).

47   Hague Conference on Private International Law (n 45), illustration 2.3.

48   *Cf* Hague Principles, Art 2(2)(b).

3   No connection is required between the law chosen and the parties or their transaction.[49]

4   The choice may be made or modified at any time. A choice or modification made after the contract has been concluded does not prejudice its formal validity or the rights of third parties.[50]

5   A choice of law cannot be contested solely on the ground that the contract to which it applies is not valid.[51]

Article 4
Choice of rules of law; incorporation by reference

1   A choice of one or more of the following instruments is recognised on the same level as the choice of the law of a country:

    (a) the UNIDROIT Principles of International Commercial Contracts;

    (b) a treaty, as defined in the United Nations Convention on the Law of Treaties;[52]

    (c) the Uniform Customs and Practice for Documentary Credits;

    (d) any instrument issued under the auspices of a regional economic integration organisation or an international, supranational or regional intergovernmental organisation,[53] including any instrument issued by the *Organisation pour l'harmonisation en Afrique du droit des affaires*.

2   If the parties choose an instrument in terms of paragraph (1)(b), (c) or (d), the UNIDROIT Principles of International

---

49   Hague Principles, Art 2(4).

50   *Cf* Hague Principles, Art 2(3); Rome I Regulation, Art 3(2).

51   Hague Principles, Art 7.

52   See DRC draft, Art 2*bis*(1)(b). The author's original version reads as follows: "an international or a regional convention, when not otherwise applicable".

53   *Cf* Hague Principles, Art 3; UNCITRAL Model Law on International Commercial Arbitration, Art 28(1). An adapted version of Art 4(1) was adopted in the DRC draft as art 2*bis*(1).

Commercial Contracts may be used in its interpretation and supplementation.[54]

3   If the parties choose the general principles of law, the *lex mercatoria*, international commercial law or the like to govern their contract, the following instruments may be applied, where relevant –

   (a)   the UNIDROIT Principles of International Commercial Contracts;[55]

   (b)   the United Nations Convention on the International Sale of Goods, as interpreted and supplemented by the UNIDROIT Principles of International Commercial Contracts;[56]

   (c)   the Uniform Customs and Practice for Documentary Credits.[57]

4   The law applicable to the contract in terms of this instrument determines whether the parties may incorporate by reference any set of rules or standard terms not listed in paragraph (1).[58]

Article 5
Express and tacit choice of law

1   A choice of law, or any modification of a choice of law, can be made expressly or tacitly.[59]

2   A tacit choice of law must be manifestly clear from the provisions of the contract, the circumstances of the case, or both.[60]

---

54   *Cf* UPICC, Preamble Par 5. See Neels and Fredericks (n 1, 2018) 350.

55   *Cf* UPICC, Preamble Par 3. See Neels and Fredericks (n 1, 2018) 350.

56   *Cf* UPICC, Preamble Par 5. See Neels and Fredericks (n 1, 2018) 350.

57   Art 4(3) was adopted in the DRC draft as Art 2*bis*(2).

58   *Cf* Rome I Regulation, Recital 13.

59   *Cf* Hague Principles, Art 4.

60   *Cf* Hague Principles, Art 4. See Jan L Neels and Eesa A Fredericks "Tacit choice of law in the Hague Principles on

3   An agreement between the parties to confer jurisdiction on a court or an arbitral tribunal to determine disputes under the contract is not in itself equivalent to a choice of law.[61]

4   An agreement between the parties to confer jurisdiction on a court or a localised arbitral tribunal may be taken into account in the determination of a tacit choice of law.[62]

Article 6
Applicable law in the absence of choice of law

1   To the extent that the law applicable to the contract has not been chosen by the parties, the law governing the contract is to be determined as follows:

   (a)   a contract for the sale of goods is governed by the law of the country of the habitual residence of the seller;

   (b)   a contract for the provision of services is governed by the law of the country of the habitual residence of the service provider;

   (c)   a contract relating to a right *in rem* in immovable property or to a tenancy of immovable property is governed by the law of the country where the property is situated;

Choice of Law in International Contracts" 2011 *De Jure* 101, 106.

61   Hague Principles, Art 4; *cf* GEDIP "Third consolidated version of a proposal to amend Articles 1, 3, 4, 5, 6, 7, 9, 10*bis*, 12 and 13 of the Rome Convention of 19 June 1980 on the Law Applicable to Contractual Obligations, and Article 15 of Regulation 44/2001 EC (Brussels I)" (Vienna, 2003) in Marc Fallon, Patrick Kinsch and Christian Kohler (eds), *Le droit international privé européen en construction. Vingt ans de travaux du GEDIP. Building European Private International Law. Twenty Years' Work by GEDIP* (Intersentia, Cambridge 2011) 425–426.

62   *Cf* Rome I Regulation, Recital 12; Hague Conference on Private International Law (n 45), Par 4.11–4.12.

(d) a franchise contract is governed by the law of the country of the habitual residence of the franchisee;

(e) a distribution contract is governed by the law of the country of the habitual residence of the distributor;

(f) a contract for the sale of goods by auction is governed by the law of the country where the auction takes place.[63]

2 Where the contract is not covered by paragraph (1) or where the elements of the contract would be covered by more than one of points (a) to (f) of paragraph (1), the contract is governed by the law of the country of the habitual residence of the party required to effect the performance which is most characteristic of the contract.

3 Where it is clear from all the circumstances of the case that the contract is manifestly more closely connected with a country other than that indicated in paragraphs (1) or (2), the contract is governed by the law of that other country.

4 Where the law applicable cannot be determined pursuant to paragraphs 1 or 2, the contract is governed by the law of the country with which it is most closely connected.[64]

Article 7
Role of international instruments

The law applicable to a contract by virtue of this instrument may be interpreted, supplemented and developed along the lines of the instruments listed in Article 4(3).[65]

---

63 *Cf* Rome I Regulation, Art 4(1)(g); DRC draft, Art 3(1)(f). Alternative solutions that may be considered include substantive-law models (Neels and Fredericks (n 1, 2018) 352-354) and the default application of the law of the country of the characteristic performance, as determined in the contract (Neels and Fredericks (n 1, 2018) 354-355).

64 Rome I Regulation, Art 4, with some substantive and linguistic changes.

65 *Cf* UPICC, Preamble Par 6; Mexico City Convention, Art 9-10. See Neels and Fredericks (n 1, 2018) 350.

Article 8
Consent and material validity; choice of law in the battle of forms

1   The existence and material validity of a contract, or of any provision in a contract, must be determined by the law which would govern it under this instrument if the contract or provision were valid.[66]

2   Nevertheless, the law of the habitual residence of a party determines whether that party has consented to the contract, or any provision in the contract, if, in the particular circumstances, it would be unreasonable to make that determination under the law specified in paragraph (1).[67]

3   If the parties have used two sets of standard terms designating different laws, or if a law is designated in one of the sets of standard terms only,[68] there is no express choice of law.[69]

Article 9
Formal validity

1   A choice of law is not subject to any requirement as to form unless otherwise agreed by the parties.[70]

2   Without prejudice to paragraph (1), a contract is formally valid if it complies with the requirements in this regard of at least one of the following legal systems:

(a)   the law of the country of the conclusion of the contract, as determined according to (i) the law of the forum, or (ii) the law applicable to the contract by virtue of this instrument;

---

66   *Cf* Rome I Regulation, Art 10(1); Hague Principles, Art 6(1)(a).
67   *Cf* Hague Principles, Art 6(2); Rome I Regulation, Art 10(2).
68   Art 6(1)(b) of the Hague Principles does not (expressly) make provision for this scenario.
69   *Cf* Hague Principles, Art 6(1)(b); Neels and Fredericks (n 1, 2018) 352 and literature referred to.
70   Hague Principles, Art 5.

    (b)   the law applicable to the contract in terms of this instrument;[71]

    (c)   the law of the country of the habitual residence of any one of the parties under the contract;

    (d)   the law of the country of the habitual residence of the agent of any one of the parties under the contract;[72]

    (e)   the law of the country of the agreed place of any substantial performance under the contract.[73]

3   As an exception to paragraph (2), but without prejudice to paragraph (1), the formal validity of a provision in a contract with the subject matter of a right *in rem* in immovable property, or of a tenancy of immovable property, is governed by the law of the country where the immovable is situated.[74]

Article 10

Renvoi

The application of the law of any country specified by this instrument entails the application of the rules of law in force in that country other than its rules of private international law, unless the parties expressly provide otherwise.[75]

Article 11

Overriding mandatory provisions

1   Overriding mandatory provisions are rules of law which are regarded as crucial by a country for safeguarding its public interests (including its political, social or economic organisation) to such an extent that they are applicable

---

71   *Cf* Hague Principles, Art 9(1)(e) and Art 9(2).
72   *Cf* Rome I Regulation, Art 11.
73   *Cf* Mexico City Convention, Art 13.
74   *Cf* Rome I Regulation, Art 11(5).
75   *Cf* Hague Principles, Art 8; Rome I Regulation, Art 20; UNCITRAL Model Law on International Commercial Arbitration, Art 28(1).

to any situation falling within their scope, irrespective of the law otherwise applicable to the contract under this instrument.

2 The overriding mandatory rules of the law governing the contract by virtue of this instrument are in principle applicable.

3 Effect may be given to the overriding mandatory rules of –

(a) the law of the forum;
(b) the law of the country of the agreed place of any substantial performance under the contract (including the country of commencement, continuation or completion of such performance).

4 In exceptional circumstances, the overriding mandatory rules of another country may be applied, provided that such law has a manifestly close connection to the particular situation.

5 In considering whether to give effect to any of the overriding mandatory rules mentioned in paragraph (3) or (4), regard must be had to their nature and purpose and to the consequences of their application or non-application.[76]

Article 12
Public policy of the forum

The application of a provision of the law applicable in terms of this instrument may be refused only if such application would

---

76 *Cf* Rome Convention, Art 7; Rome I Regulation, Art 9; Hague Principles, Art 11(1), (2) and (5). The reference to par 3 and 4 in Art 11(5) should perhaps be limited to par 3(b) and 4: see Jan L Neels and Eesa A Fredericks "Covid-19 regulations as overriding mandatory provisions in private international law – a comparison of regional, supranational and international instruments with the proposed African Principles on the Law Applicable to International Commercial Contracts" in Murdoch Watney (ed) *The Impact of COVID-19 on the Future of Law and Related Disciplines* (UJ Press, 2022) 1 at 14 n 78.

be manifestly incompatible with fundamental notions of the public policy of the forum.[77]

Article 13
Scope of the law applicable to the contract

1   The law applicable to a contract by virtue of this instrument governs all aspects of the contract between the parties, including but not limited to –

(a) interpretation;[78]

(b) rights and obligations arising from the contract;[79]

(c) the various ways of extinguishing obligations, and prescription and limitation periods;[80]

(d) the consequences of the formal or material invalidity of the contract;[81]

(e) burden of proof and legal presumptions;[82]

(f) pre-contractual obligations.[83]

2

(a) The law applicable to the contract by virtue of this instrument governs performance[84] and the consequences of a total or partial breach of obligations, including the assessment of damages[85] in as far as such is governed by rules of law.[86]

---

77   *Cf* Rome I Regulation, Art 21; Hague Principles, Art 11(3)-(5).

78   Hague Principles, Art 9(1)(a); Rome I Regulation, Art 12(1)(a).

79   Hague Principles, Art 9(1)(b).

80   Hague Principles, Art 9(1)(d); *cf* Rome I Regulation, Art 12(1)(d).

81   *Cf* Hague Principles, Art 9(1)(e); Rome I Regulation, Art 12(1)(e).

82   Hague Principles, Art 9(1)(f); *cf* Rome I Regulation, Art 18(1).

83   Hague Principles, Art 9(1)(g).

84   Hague Principles, Art 9(1)(c); Rome I Regulation, Art 12(1)(b).

85   *Cf* Hague Principles art 9(1)(c); Rome I Regulation, Art 12(1)(c).

86   *Cf* Rome I Regulation, Art 12(1)(c).

(b) However, a court or arbitral tribunal may refuse to award damages in terms of the law applicable by virtue of paragraph (a) to the extent that the damages would exceed compensation for actual loss (exemplary or punitive damages).[87]

(c) Nevertheless, a court or arbitral tribunal must take into account whether and to what extent exemplary or punitive damages in terms of the law applicable to the contract serve to cover costs and expenses relating to the procedure.[88]

(d) In relation to the manner of performance and the steps to be taken in the event of defective performance, the law of the country of the agreed place of performance must be taken into account.[89]

Article 14
Set-off

Set-off is governed by the law applicable to the claim against which the right to set-off is asserted, unless otherwise agreed by the parties.[90]

Article 15
Habitual residence

1 For the purposes of this instrument, the habitual residence of companies and other bodies, corporate or unincorporated, is in the country of their central administration.[91]

---

87 See Rome II Regulation, Recital 32; *cf* Hague Convention on Choice of Court Agreements, Art 11(1); Hague Convention on the Recognition and Enforcement of Foreign Judgments in Civil or Commercial Matters, Art 10(1).

88 *Cf* Hague Convention on Choice of Court Agreements, Art 11(2); Hague Convention on the Recognition and Enforcement of Foreign Judgments in Civil or Commercial Matters, Art 10(2).

89 Rome I Regulation, Art 12(2).

90 *Cf* Rome I Regulation, Art 17.

91 *Cf* Rome I Regulation, Art 19(1).

2   The habitual residence of a natural person acting in the course of his or her business activities is in the country of his or her principal place of business.[92]

3   Where the contract is concluded in the course of the operations of a branch, agency or any other establishment, or if, under the contract, performance is the responsibility of such a branch, agency or establishment, the country where the branch, agency or any other establishment is located must be treated as the country of habitual residence.[93]

4   For the purposes of determining habitual residence, the relevant point in time is the moment of the conclusion of the contract.[94]

Article 16
Interpretation and uniformity of application

In the interpretation of this instrument, its regional character and international relevance, and the need to promote uniformity in its application must be taken into account.[95]

Article 17
Entry into force and application in time

This instrument was adopted by the African Union on [date] and applies to contracts concluded as from [date]. In disputes relating to contracts concluded prior to this date, the court or arbitral tribunal may take the provisions of this instrument into account.[96]

---

92   *Cf* Rome I Regulation, Art 19(1); Fredericks (n 35) 248.
93   *Cf* Rome I Regulation, Art 19(2); Hague Principles, Art 12.
94   *Cf* Rome I Regulation, Art 19(3).
95   *Cf* CISG, Art 7(1); Mexico City Convention, Art 4; Hague Convention on Choice of Court Agreements, Art 23; Hague Convention on the Recognition and Enforcement of Foreign Judgments in Civil or Commercial Matters, Art 20.
96   For the second sentence, see DRC draft, Art 24 (second sentence).

Principes africains sur le droit applicable aux contrats commerciaux internationaux

*Translation in French by Dr Justin Monsenepwo**

Préambule

1. Le présent instrument énonce les principes généraux pour déterminer le droit applicable aux contrats commerciaux internationaux.[97]

2. Ils peuvent servir de modèle pour les instruments législatifs nationaux, régionaux et supranationaux en Afrique.[98]

3. Ils peuvent être utilisés par les tribunaux africains pour interpréter, compléter et élaborer des règles de droit international privé sur les contrats.[99]

4. Ils peuvent être utilisés par les tribunaux arbitraux pour interpréter, compléter et élaborer des règles de droit international privé sur les contrats lorsque cela est approprié et si le tribunal a son siège en Afrique ou ailleurs.[100]

---

* Attorney, Wick Phillips Gould & Martin, LLP, Dallas (Texas, USA); research associate, University of Oxford (United Kingdom) and Research Centre for Private International Law in Emerging Countries, Faculty of Law, University of Johannesburg (South Africa).

96 Cf. Principes de La Haye, Préambule, para. 1 ; Principes d'UNIDROIT relatifs aux contrats du commerce international, Préambule, para. 1.

98 Cf. Principes de La Haye, Préambule, para. 2.

99 Cf. Principes de La Haye, Préambule, para. 3 et 4 ; UPICC, Préambule, para. 5 et 6.

100 Cf. Principes de La Haye, Préambule, para. 3 et 4.

Article 1
Champ d'application des Principes

1. Ces Principes s'appliquent, dans les situations de conflit de lois, aux obligations contractuelles internationales en matière civile et commerciale, lorsque chaque partie agit dans l'exercice de son commerce ou de sa profession.[101]

2. Ces principes ne traitent pas de la loi régissant les types de contrats suivants :

    (a) les contrats de consommation ;[102]
    (b) les contrats de transport ;[103]
    (c) les contrats de travail ;[104]
    (d) les contrats d'assurance.[105]

3. Ces principes ne traitent pas de la loi régissant les conventions d'arbitrage et d'élection de for.[106]

4. Ces principes ne traitent pas de la loi régissant les sujets suivants :

    (a) la capacité des personnes physiques ;[107]
    (b) les sociétés ou autres groupements et les trusts ;[108]
    (c) la preuve et la procédure ;[109]

---

101 Cf. Principes de La Haye, article 1(1) ; Règlement Rome I, article 1(1).

102 Cf. Principes de La Haye, article 1(1). Voir l'arrangement spécifique à l'article 6 du Règlement Rome I.

103 Voir l'arrangement spécifique à l'article 5 du Règlement Rome I.

104 Voir l'arrangement spécifique à l'article 8 du Règlement Rome I.

105 Voir l'arrangement spécifique à l'article 7 du Règlement Rome I.

106 Cf. Principes de La Haye, article 1(3)(b) ; Règlement Rome I, article 1(2)(e).

107 Cf. Principes de La Haye, article 1(3)(a) ; Règlement Rome I, article 1(2)(a). Voir article 13 du Règlement Rome I pour une règle de conflit de lois partielle sur la capacité contractuelle d'une personne physique. Pour une proposition alternative sur ce sujet, voir Fredericks (n 35) 248-249.

108 Cf. Principes de La Haye article 1(3)(c) ; Règlement Rome I, article 1(2)(f).

109 Cf. Règlement Rome I article 1(3).

(d) l'insolvabilité ;[110]

(e) la question de savoir si un représentant peut engager, envers les tiers, la personne pour le compte de laquelle il prétend agir ;[111]

(f) les instruments négociables ;[112]

(g) les effets patrimoniaux des contrats ;[113]

(h) les matières fiscales, douanières et administratives.[114]

Article 2
Application universelle

La loi désignée par le présent instrument est applicable, qu'il s'agisse ou non du droit d'un État membre de l'Union africaine.[115]

Article 3
Liberté de choix

1. Le contrat est régi par la loi choisie par les parties.[116]

2. Les parties peuvent choisir :

(a) la loi applicable à l'ensemble du contrat ou à un ou plusieurs aspects[117] ou parties de celui-ci ;[118] et

---

110 Cf. Principes de La Haye article 1(3)(d) ; Règlement Rome I, article 1(2)(f).

111 Cf. Principes de La Haye, article 1(3)(f) ; Règlement Rome I, article 1(2)(g).

112 Cf. Règlement Rome I, article 1(2)(d).

113 Cf. Principes de La Haye, article 1(3)(e).

114 Cf. Règlement Rome I, article 1(1).

115 Cf. Règlement Rome I, article 2.

116 Principes de La Haye, article 2(1) ; cf. Règlement Rome I, article 3(1) ; Loi type de la CNUDCI sur l'arbitrage commercial international, article 28(1).

117 Conférence de La Haye de droit international privé, *Principes sur le choix du droit dans les contrats commerciaux internationaux* (HCCH, La Haye 2015) (Commentaire officiel relatif aux Principes de La Haye), illustration 2.2.

118 Cf. Principes de La Haye, article 2(2)(a) ; Règlement Rome I, article 3(1).

(b) des lois différentes pour différents aspects[119] ou parties du contrat.[120]

3. Aucun lien n'est requis entre la loi choisie et les parties ou leur transaction.[121]

4. Le choix peut être fait ou modifié à tout moment. Un choix ou une modification effectuée après la conclusion du contrat ne porte atteinte ni à sa validité formelle ni aux droits de tiers.[122]

5. Le choix de la loi applicable ne peut être contesté au seul motif que le contrat auquel il s'applique n'est pas valable.[123]

Article 4
Choix des règles de droit ; incorporation par référence

1. Le choix d'un ou de plusieurs des instruments suivants est reconnu au même titre que le choix de la loi d'un pays :

(a) les Principes d'UNIDROIT relatifs aux contrats du commerce international;

(b) un traité, tel que défini par la Convention des Nations Unies sur le droit des traités ;[124]

(c) les Règles et Usances Uniformes ;

(d) tout instrument adopté sous les auspices d'une organisation régionale d'intégration économique ou d'une organisation intergouvernementale internationale, supranationale ou régionale,[125]

---

119 Conférence de La Haye de droit international privé (n 117), illustration 2.3.

120 Cf. Principes de La Haye, article 2(2)(b).

121 Principes de La Haye, article 2(4).

122 Cf. Principes de La Haye, article 2(3) ; Règlement Rome I, article 3(2).

123 Principes de La Haye, article 7.

124 Voir l'Avant-projet de la RDC, article 2*bis*(1)(b). La version originale dispose : « une convention internationale ou régionale, lorsqu'elle n'est pas autrement applicable ».

125 Cf. Principes de La Haye, article 3 ; Loi type de la CNUDCI sur l'arbitrage commercial international, article 28(1). Une

notamment tout instrument émanant de l'Organisation pour l'harmonisation en Afrique du droit des affaires.

2. Si les parties choisissent un instrument aux termes du paragraphe (1)(b), (c) ou (d), les Principes d'UNIDROIT relatifs aux contrats du commerce international peuvent être utilisés pour interpréter et compléter cet instrument.[126]

3. Si les parties choisissent les principes généraux du droit, la *lex mercatoria*, le droit commercial international ou d'autres règles de droit semblables pour régir leur contrat, les instruments suivants peuvent être appliqués, le cas échéant :

    (a) les Principes d'UNIDROIT relatifs aux contrats du commerce international ;[127]

    (b) la Convention des Nations unies sur les contrats de vente internationale de marchandises, telle qu'interprétée et complétée par les Principes d'UNIDROIT relatifs aux contrats du commerce international ;[128]

    (c) les Règles et Usances Uniformes.[129]

4. La loi applicable au contrat aux termes du présent instrument détermine si les parties peuvent intégrer par référence un ensemble de règles ou de conditions générales non énumérées au paragraphe 1.[130]

---

version adaptée de l'article 4(1) a été adoptée dans l'Avant-projet de la RDC à l'article 2*bis*(1).

126 Cf. Principes d'UNIDROIT relatifs aux contrats du commerce international, Préambule, para. 5. Voir Neels et Fredericks (n 1, 2018) 350.

127 Cf. Principes d'UNIDROIT relatifs aux contrats du commerce international, Préambule, para. 3. Voir Neels et Fredericks (n 1, 2018) 350.

128 Cf. Principes d'UNIDROIT relatifs aux contrats du commerce international, Préambule, para. 5. Voir Neels et Fredericks (n 1, 2018) 350.

129 L'article 4(3) fut adopté dans l'Avant-projet de la RDC à l'article 2*bis*(2).

130 Cf. Rome I Règlement, Préambule, para. 13.

Article 5
Choix exprès et tacite

1. Le choix de la loi applicable, ou toute modification du choix de la loi applicable, peut être fait de façon expresse ou tacite.[131]

2. Le choix tacite de la loi applicable doit résulter manifestement des dispositions du contrat ou des circonstances de l'affaire, ou des deux.[132]

3. Un accord entre les parties visant à donner compétence à un tribunal étatique ou arbitral pour connaître des différends liés au contrat n'est pas en soi équivalent à un choix de la loi applicable.[133]

4. Un accord entre les parties visant à donner compétence à un tribunal étatique ou à un tribunal arbitral déterminé peut être pris en compte dans la détermination du choix tacite de la loi applicable.[134]

Article 6
Droit applicable à défaut de choix

1. Dans la mesure où la loi applicable au contrat n'a pas été choisie par les parties, la loi régissant le contrat est déterminée comme suit :

   (a) le contrat de vente de biens est régi par la loi du pays dans lequel le vendeur a sa résidence habituelle ;

   (b) le contrat de prestation de services est régi par la loi du pays dans lequel le prestataire de services a sa résidence habituelle ;

   (c) le contrat ayant pour objet un droit réel immobilier ou un bail d'immeuble est régi par la loi du pays dans lequel est situé l'immeuble ;

---

131   Cf. Principes de La Haye, article 4.

132   Cf. Principes de La Haye, article 4. Voir Neels et Fredericks (n 60) 106.

133   Principe de La Hayes, article 4. Cf. GEDIP / Fallon, Kinsch et Kohler (eds) (n 61) 425-426.

134   Cf. Règlement Rome I, Préambule, para. 12 ; Conférence de La Haye de droit international privé (n 117), para. 4.11-4.12.

(d) le contrat de franchise est régi par la loi du pays dans lequel le franchisé a sa résidence habituelle ;

(e) le contrat de distribution est régi par la loi du pays dans lequel le distributeur a sa résidence habituelle ;

(f) le contrat de vente de biens aux enchères est régi par la loi du pays où la vente aux enchères a lieu.[135]

2. Lorsque le contrat n'est pas couvert par le paragraphe 1 ou lorsque les éléments du contrat sont couverts par plusieurs des points (a) à (f) du paragraphe 1, le contrat est régi par la loi du pays dans lequel la partie qui doit fournir la prestation caractéristique a sa résidence habituelle.

3. Lorsqu'il résulte clairement de l'ensemble des circonstances de la cause que le contrat présente des liens manifestement plus étroits avec un pays autre que celui visé au paragraphe 1 ou 2, la loi de cet autre pays s'applique.

4. Lorsque la loi applicable ne peut être déterminée sur la base du paragraphe 1 ou 2, le contrat est régi par la loi du pays avec lequel il présente les liens les plus étroits.[136]

Article 7
Rôle des instruments internationaux

La loi applicable à un contrat en vertu de cet instrument peut être interprétée, complétée et développée conformément aux instruments énumérés à l'article 4(3).[137]

---

135 Cf. Règlement Rome I, article 4(1)(g) ; Avant-projet de la RDC, article 3(1)(f). Parmi les solutions alternatives qui peuvent être envisagées figurent les modèles de droit substantiel (Neels et Fredericks (n 1, 2018) 352-354) et l'application par défaut de la loi du pays de la prestation caractéristique déterminée dans le contrat (Neels et Fredericks (n 1, 2018) 354-355).

136 Règlement Rome I, article 4, avec quelques modifications substantielles et linguistiques.

137 Cf. Principes d'UNIDROIT relatifs aux contrats du commerce international, Préambule, para. 6 ; Convention de Mexico, articles 9 et 10. Voir Neels et Fredericks (n 1, 2018) 350.

Article 8
Consentement et validité matérielle ; choix de la loi applicable en cas de conflit de conditions générales

1. L'existence et la validité matérielle d'un contrat, ou de toute clause de celui-ci sont déterminées par la loi qui le régirait en vertu du présent instrument si le contrat ou la clause étaient valables.[138]
2. Toutefois, la loi du pays dans lequel une partie a sa résidence habituelle détermine si cette partie a consenti au contrat ou toute disposition de celui-ci, si, dans les circonstances particulières de la cause, il ne serait pas raisonnable de déterminer l'effet du comportement de cette partie en vertu de la loi prévue au paragraphe (1).[139]
3. Si les parties ont eu recours à des conditions générales qui désignent des lois différentes, ou si une loi est désignée dans l'un des ensembles de conditions générales seulement,[140] il n'y a pas le choix exprès de la loi applicable.[141]

Article 9
Validité formelle

1. Le choix de la loi applicable n'est soumis à aucune condition de forme, sauf convention contraire des parties.[142]
2. Sans préjudice du paragraphe 1, le contrat est valable quant à la forme s'il satisfait aux exigences à cet égard d'au moins un des systèmes juridiques suivants :

---

138 Cf. Règlement Rome I, article 10(1) ; Principes de La Haye, article 6(1)a).
139 Cf. Principes de La Haye, article 6(2) ; Règlement Rome I, article 10(2).
140 L'article 6(1)(b) des Principes de La Haye ne prévoit pas (expressément) ce scénario.
141 Cf. Principes de La Haye, article 6(1)(b) ; Neels et Fredericks (n 1, 2018) 352 et la littérature y mentionnée.
142 Principes de La Haye, article 5.

(a) la loi du pays de la conclusion du contrat, telle que déterminée en vertu (i) de la loi du juge saisi, ou (ii) la loi applicable au contrat en vertu du présent instrument ;

(b) la loi applicable au contrat aux termes du présent instrument ;[143]

(c) la loi du pays de résidence habituelle de l'une ou l'autre des parties au contrat ;

(d) la loi du pays de résidence habituelle de l'agent de l'une ou l'autre des parties au contrat ;[144]

(e) la loi du pays du lieu convenu pour toute prestation substantielle en vertu du contrat.[145]

3. Par exception au paragraphe 2, mais sans préjudice du paragraphe 1, la validité formelle de la disposition d'un contrat ayant pour objet un droit réel immobilier ou un bail d'immeuble est régie par le droit du pays où se trouve l'immeuble.[146]

Article 10
Renvoi

L'application de la loi de tout pays désigné par cet instrument implique l'application des règles de droit en vigueur dans ce pays autres que ses règles de droit international privé, sauf si les parties conviennent expressément du contraire.[147]

Article 11
Lois de police

1. Les lois de police sont des règles de droit qui sont considérées comme cruciales par un pays pour la

---

143 Cf. Principes de La Haye, articles 9(1)(e) et 9(2).
144 Cf. Règlement Rome I, article 11.
145 Cf. Convention de Mexico, article 13.
146 Cf. Règlement Rome I, article 11(5).
147 Cf. Principes de La Haye, article 8 ; Règlement Rome I, article 20 ; Loi type de la CNUDCI sur l'arbitrage commercial international, article 28(1).

sauvegarde de ses intérêts publics (y compris son organisation politique, sociale ou économique), dans la mesure où elles sont applicables à toute situation relevant de leur champ d'application, quelle que soit la loi autrement applicable au contrat aux termes du présent instrument.

2. Les lois de police de la loi régissant le contrat en vertu du présent instrument sont en principe applicables.

3. Il pourra également être donné effet aux lois de police de :

   (a) la loi du for ;
   (b) la loi du pays du lieu convenu pour l'exécution des obligations substantielles découlant du contrat (y compris le pays du commencement, de la poursuite ou de l'achèvement de cette exécution).

4. Dans des circonstances exceptionnelles, il pourra également être donné effet aux lois de police d'un autre pays, à condition que cette loi ait un lien manifestement étroit avec la cause.

5. Pour décider si effet doit être donné aux lois de police mentionnées aux paragraphes 3 et 4, il est tenu compte de leur nature et de leur objet, ainsi que des conséquences de leur application ou de leur non-application.[148]

Article 12
Ordre public du for

L'application d'une disposition de la loi applicable aux termes du présent instrument ne peut être écartée que si cette application est manifestement incompatible avec les notions fondamentales de l'ordre public du for.[149]

---

148   Cf. Convention de Rome, article 7 ; Règlement Rome I, article 9; Principes de La Haye, article 11(1), (2) et (5).
149   Cf. Règlement Rome I, article 21 ; Principes de La Haye, article 11(3)-(5).

Article 13
Domaine de la loi applicable au contrat

1. La loi applicable à un contrat en vertu du présent instrument régit tous les aspects du contrat entre les parties, notamment :

    (a) son interprétation ;[150]
    (b) les droits et obligations que le contrat engendre ;[151]
    (c) les diverses façons d'éteindre les obligations, ainsi que les délais de prescription et de prescription ;[152]
    (d) les conséquences de l'invalidité formelle ou matérielle du contrat ;[153]
    (e) la charge de la preuve et les présomptions ;[154]
    (f) les obligations précontractuelles.[155]

2.

    (a) La loi applicable au contrat en vertu du présent instrument régit l'exécution[156] des obligations et les conséquences de l'inexécution totale ou partielle de ces obligations, y compris l'évaluation du dommage[157] dans la mesure où des règles de droit la gouvernent.[158]
    (b) Toutefois, le tribunal étatique ou arbitral peut refuser d'accorder des dommages-intérêts en vertu de la loi applicable en vertu du paragraphe (a) dans

---

150   Principes de La Haye, article 9(1)a) ; Règlement Rome I, article 12(1)a).

151   Principes de La Haye, article 9(1)(b).

152   Principes de La Haye, article 9(1)(d) ; cf. Règlement Rome I, article 12(1)(d).

153   Cf. Principes de La Haye, article 9(1)(e) ; Règlement Rome I, article 12(1)(e).

154   Principes de La Haye, article 9(1)(f) ; cf. Règlement Rome I, article 18(1).

155   Principes de La Haye, article 9(1)(g).

156   Principes de La Haye, article 9(1)(c) ; Règlement Rome I, article 12(1)(b).

157   Cf. Hague Principles, article 9(1)(c) ; Règlement Rome I, article 12(1)(c).

158   Cf. Règlement Rome I, article 12(1)(c).

la mesure où les dommages-intérêts dépasseraient l'indemnisation pour perte réelle (dommages-intérêts exemplaires ou punitifs).[159]

(c) Néanmoins, le tribunal étatique ou arbitral doit tenir compte de la question de savoir si et dans quelle mesure les dommages-intérêts exemplaires ou punitifs aux termes de la loi applicable au contrat servent à couvrir les coûts et les dépenses liés à la procédure.[160]

(d) En ce qui concerne les modalités d'exécution et les mesures à prendre en cas de défaut dans l'exécution, il est tenu compte de la loi du pays du lieu d'exécution convenu.[161]

Article 14
Compensation

Sauf accord contraire des parties, la compensation est régie par la loi applicable à l'obligation contre laquelle elle est invoquée.[162]

Article 15
Résidence habituelle

1. Aux fins du présent instrument, la résidence habituelle d'une société, association ou personne morale est le lieu où elle a établi son administration centrale.[163]

---

159 Voir Règlement Rome II, Préambule para. 32 ; cf. Convention de La Haye sur les accords d'élection de for, article 11(1) ; Convention de La Haye sur la reconnaissance et l'exécution des jugements étrangers en matière civile ou commerciale, article 10(1).

160 Cf. Convention de La Haye sur les accords d'élection de for, article 11(2) ; Convention de La Haye sur la reconnaissance et l'exécution des jugements étrangers en matière civile ou commerciale, article 10(2).

161 Règlement Rome I, article 12(2).

162 Cf. Règlement Rome I, article 17.

163 Cf. Règlement Rome I, article 19(1).

2. La résidence habituelle d'une personne physique agissant dans l'exercice de son activité professionnelle est le lieu où cette personne a son établissement principal.[164]

3. Lorsque le contrat est conclu dans le cadre de l'exploitation d'une succursale, d'une agence ou de tout autre établissement, ou si, selon le contrat, la prestation doit être fournie par lesdits succursale, agence ou autre établissement, le lieu où est situé cette succursale, cette agence ou tout autre établissement est traité comme résidence habituelle.[165]

4. La résidence habituelle est déterminée au moment de la conclusion du contrat.[166]

Article 16
Interprétation et uniformité d'application

Dans l'interprétation du présent instrument, il est tenu compte de son caractère régional, de sa pertinence internationale, et de la nécessité de promouvoir l'uniformité de son application.[167]

Article 17
Entrée en vigueur et application dans le temps

Le présent instrument a été adopté par le Union Africaine [date] et s'applique aux contrats conclus à partir de [date]. Pour les litiges relatifs aux contrats conclus avant cette date, le tribunal étatique ou arbitral peut tenir compte des dispositions du présent instrument.[168]

---

164 Cf. Règlement Rome I, article 19(1) ; Fredericks (n 35) 248.

165 Cf. Règlement Rome I, article 19(2) ; Principes de La Haye, article 12.

166 Cf. Règlement Rome I, article 19(3).

167 Cf. Convention des Nations Unies sur les contrats de vente internationale de marchandises, article 7(1) ; Convention de Mexico, article 4 ; Convention de La Haye sur les accords d'élection de for, article 23 ; Convention de La Haye sur la reconnaissance et l'exécution des jugements étrangers en matière civile ou commerciale, article 20.

168 Pour ce qui est de la deuxième phrase, voir l'Avant-projet de la RDC, article 24 (deuxième phrase).

Princípios Africanos relativos à Lei Aplicável aos Contratos Comerciais Internacionais

Translation in Portuguese by Prof Rui Dias and Ms Rita Duarte***

Preâmbulo

1. O presente instrumento estabelece princípios gerais para a determinação da lei aplicável aos contratos comerciais internacionais[169].

2. Os princípios podem ser usados como modelo para instrumentos legislativos nacionais, regionais e supranacionais em África[170].

3. Os princípios podem ser usados por tribunais africanos para interpretar, complementar ou desenvolver normas de direito internacional privado relativas a contratos[171].

4. Os princípios podem ser usados por tribunais arbitrais para interpretar, complementar ou desenvolver normas de direito internacional privado relativas a contratos, sempre que apropriado e quer o tribunal esteja sediado em África ou noutro lugar[172].

---

* Professor of Law, Faculty of Law, University of Coimbra.
** LLM candidate at the College of Europe, Bruges.

168 Cf. Princípios da Haia relativos à Escolha de Lei Aplicável a Contratos Comerciais Internacionais, Preâmbulo, Parágrafo 1; Princípios da UNIDROIT sobre Contratos Comerciais Internacionais, Preâmbulo, Parágrafo 1.

170 Cf. Princípios da Haia, Preâmbulo, Par. 2.

171 Cf. Princípios da Haia, Preâmbulo, Par. 3 e 4; Princípios da UNIDROIT, Par. 5 e 6.

172 Cf. Princípios da Haia, Preâmbulo, Par. 3 e 4.

Artigo 1.º
Âmbito de aplicação dos princípios

1. Os presentes princípios aplicam-se, em situações que impliquem um conflito de leis, a obrigações contratuais internacionais em matéria civil e comercial, em que cada parte atue no exercício da sua atividade comercial ou profissional[173].

2. Os presentes princípios não se aplicam à determinação da lei que regula as seguintes categorias de contratos:

    (a) contratos celebrados por consumidores[174];
    (b) contratos de transporte[175];
    (c) contratos de trabalho[176];
    (d) contratos de seguro[177].

3. Os presentes princípios não se aplicam à determinação da lei que regula as convenções de arbitragem e de eleição do foro[178].

4. Os presentes princípios não se aplicam à determinação da lei que regula:

    (a) a capacidade das pessoas singulares[179];
    (b) sociedades ou outras entidades e *trusts*[180];
    (c) prova e processo[181];

---

173 Cf. Princípios da Haia, Art. 1º, nº 1; Regulamento Roma I, Art. 1º, nº 1.

174 Cf. Princípios da Haia, Art. 1º, nº 1; v. a disposição específica do Art. 6º do Regulamento Roma I.

175 V. a disposição específica do Art. 5º do Regulamento Roma I.

176 V. a disposição específica do Art. 8º do Regulamento Roma I.

177 V. a disposição específica do Art. 7º do Regulamento Roma I.

178 Cf. Princípios da Haia, Art. 1º, nº 3, al. b); Regulamento Roma I, Art. 1º, nº 2, al. e).

179 Cf. Princípios da Haia, Art. 1º, nº 3, al. a); Regulamento Roma I, Art. 1º, nº 2, al. a). V. Art. 13º do Regulamento Roma I para uma norma parcial de conflitos relativa à capacidade contratual de uma pessoa singular. Para uma proposta alternativa neste âmbito, v. Fredericks (n 35) pp. 248-249.

180 Cf. Princípios da Haia, Art. 1º, nº 3, al. c); Regulamento Roma I, Art. 1º, nº 2, al. f).

181 Cf. Regulamento Roma I, Art. 1º, nº 3.

(d) insolvência[182];

(e) a questão de saber se um agente pode vincular, em relação a terceiros, a pessoa por conta da qual pretende agir[183];

(f) títulos negociáveis[184];

(g) os efeitos reais dos contratos[185];

(h) matérias fiscais, aduaneiras e administrativas[186].

Artigo 2.º
Aplicação universal

A lei designada pelo presente instrumento é aplicável mesmo que não seja a lei de um Estado membro da União Africana[187].

Artigo 3.º
Liberdade de escolha da lei

1. O contrato rege-se pela lei escolhida pelas partes[188].

2. As partes podem designar:

(a) a lei aplicável à totalidade do contrato ou a um ou mais aspetos[189] ou partes do mesmo[190]; e

---

182 Cf. Princípios da Haia, Art. 1º, nº 3, al. d); Regulamento Roma I, Art. 1º, nº 2, al. f).

183 Cf. Princípios da Haia, Art. 1º, nº 3, al. f); Regulamento Roma I, Art. 1º, nº 2, al. g).

184 Cf. Regulamento Roma I, Art. 1º, nº 2, al. d).

185 Cf. Princípios da Haia, Art. 1º, nº 3, al. e).

186 Cf. Regulamento Roma I, Art. 1º, nº 1.

187 Cf. Regulamento Roma I, Art. 2º.

188 Cf. Princípios da Haia, Art. 2º, nº 1; Regulamento Roma I, Art. 3º, nº 1; Lei Modelo da UNCITRAL sobre Arbitragem Comercial Internacional, Art. 28º, nº1.

189 Conferência da Haia de Direito Internacional Privado, Comentários sobre os Princípios relativos à Escolha de Lei Aplicável aos Contratos Comerciais Internacionais, Haia, 2015, Ponto 2.2.

190 Cf. Princípios da Haia, Art. 2º, nº 2, al. a); Regulamento Roma I, Art. 3º, nº 1.

(b) diferentes leis para diferentes aspetos[191] ou partes do contrato[192].

3. Não é exigível qualquer conexão entre a lei aplicável e as partes ou a sua transação[193].

4. A escolha pode ser feita ou modificada a todo o tempo. Uma escolha ou modificação posterior à celebração do contrato não afeta a sua validade formal nem prejudica os direitos de terceiros[194].

5. Uma escolha de lei não pode ser contestada apenas com base na invalidade do contrato a que se aplica[195].

Artigo 4.º
Escolha de normas jurídicas; inclusão por remissão

1. A escolha de um ou mais dos seguintes instrumentos é reconhecida ao mesmo nível que a escolha de uma lei nacional:

(a) Princípios UNIDROIT sobre Contratos Comerciais Internacionais;

(b) um tratado, tal como definido na Convenção das Nações Unidas sobre o Direito dos Tratados[196];

(c) Regras e Usos Uniformes relativos a Créditos Documentários;

(d) qualquer instrumento emitido no seio de uma organização regional de integração económica ou de uma organização intergovernamental internacional,

---

191 Conferência da Haia de Direito Internacional Privado, *cit.*, Ponto 2.3.

192 Cf. Princípios da Haia, Art. 2º, nº 2, al. b).

193 Cf. Princípios da Haia, Art. 2º, nº 4.

194 Cf. Princípios da Haia, Art. 2º, nº 3; Regulamento Roma I, Art. 3º, nº 2.

195 Cf. Princípios da Haia, Art. 7º.

196 V. Projeto de Lei relativa à Lei Aplicável às Obrigações Contratuais da República Democrática do Congo, Art. 2º*bis*, nº 1, al. b). Na versão original lia-se: "uma convenção internacional ou regional, quando não aplicável de outra forma".

supranacional ou regional[197], incluindo qualquer instrumento emitido pela *Organisation pour l'harmonisation en Afrique du droit des affaires.*

2. Se as partes escolherem um instrumento nos termos do nº 1, al. b), c) ou d), os Princípios UNIDROIT sobre Contratos Comerciais Internacionais podem ser usados na sua interpretação e complementação[198].

3. Se as partes escolherem os princípios gerais de Direito, a *lex mercatoria*, direito comercial internacional ou semelhante para reger o contrato, podem ser aplicados os seguintes instrumentos, quando relevante:

    (a) Princípios UNIDROIT sobre Contratos Comerciais Internacionais[199];

    (b) A Convenção das Nações Unidas sobre Contratos para Venda Internacional de Mercadorias, interpretada e complementada pelos Princípios UNIDROIT sobre Contratos Comerciais Internacionais[200];

    (c) Regras e Usos Uniformes relativos a Créditos Documentários[201].

4. A lei aplicável ao contrato nos termos do presente instrumento determina se as partes podem incluir, por

---

197 Cf. Princípios da Haia, Art. 3º; Lei Modelo da UNCITRAL sobre Arbitragem Comercial Internacional, Art. 28º, nº1. Uma versão adaptada do Art. 4º, nº1, foi adotada no Projeto de Lei da República Democrática do Congo no Artigo 2º*bis*, nº1.

198 Cf. Princípios da UNIDROIT sobre Contratos Comerciais Internacionais, Preâmbulo, Par. 5. V. Neels e Fredericks (n 1, 2018) p. 350.

199 Cf. Princípios da UNIDROIT sobre Contratos Comerciais Internacionais, Preâmbulo, Par. 3. V. Neels e Fredericks, *op. cit.*, p. 350.

200 Cf. Princípios da UNIDROIT sobre Contratos Comerciais Internacionais, Preâmbulo, Par. 5. V. Neels e Fredericks, *op. cit.*, p. 350.

201 O Art. 4º, nº3, foi adotado no Projeto de Lei da República Democrática do Congo como Art. 2º*bis*, nº 2.

remissão, qualquer conjunto de regras ou cláusulas contratuais gerais não enumeradas no nº1[202].

Artigo 5.º
Escolha de lei expressa e tácita

1. A escolha de lei, ou qualquer modificação da escolha de lei, pode ser efetuada expressa ou tacitamente[203].
2. A escolha tácita de lei deve resultar de forma clara das cláusulas do contrato, das circunstâncias do caso, ou de ambas[204].
3. Uma convenção de arbitragem ou de eleição do foro para decidir litígios decorrentes do contrato não é, por si só, equivalente a uma escolha de lei[205].
4. Uma convenção de arbitragem ou de eleição do foro pode ser tida em consideração para a determinação de uma escolha tácita de lei[206].

Artigo 6.º
Lei aplicável na falta de escolha de lei

1. Se a lei aplicável não tiver sido escolhida pelas partes, a lei aplicável ao contrato é determinada do seguinte modo:

    (a) o contrato de compra e venda de mercadorias é regulado pela lei do país em que o vendedor tem a sua residência habitual;

    (b) o contrato de prestação de serviços é regulado pela lei do país em que o prestador de serviços tem a sua residência habitual;

    (c) o contrato que tem por objeto um direito real sobre um bem imóvel ou o arrendamento de um bem

---

202　Cf. Regulamento Roma I, considerando nº 13.
203　Cf. Princípios da Haia, Art. 4º.
204　Cf. Princípios da Haia, Art. 4º. V. Neels e Fredericks (n 60) p. 106.
205　Cf. Princípios da Haia, Art. 4º; GEDIP / Fallon, Kinsch e Kohler (coord.) (n 61) pp. 425-426.
206　Cf. Regulamento Roma I, considerando nº 12; Conferência da Haia de Direito Internacional Privado, *cit.*, Pontos 4.11-4.12.

> imóvel é regulado pela lei do país onde o imóvel se situa;
>
> (d) o contrato de franquia é regulado pela lei do país em que o franqueado tem a sua residência habitual;
>
> (e) o contrato de distribuição é regulado pela lei do país em que o distribuidor tem a sua residência habitual;
>
> (f) o contrato de compra e venda de mercadorias em hasta pública é regulado pela lei do país em que se realiza a compra e venda em hasta pública[207].

2. Caso o contrato não seja abrangido pelo nº 1, ou se partes do contrato forem abrangidas por mais do que uma das alíneas a) a f) do nº 1, o contrato é regulado pela lei do país em que o contraente que deve efetuar a prestação característica do contrato tem a sua residência habitual.

3. Caso resulte claramente do conjunto das circunstâncias do caso que o contrato apresenta uma conexão manifestamente mais estreita com um país diferente do indicado nos nᵒˢ 1 ou 2, é aplicável a lei desse outro país.

4. Caso a lei aplicável não possa ser determinada em aplicação do nº 1 ou do nº 2, o contrato é regulado pela lei do país com o qual apresenta uma conexão mais estreita[208].

Artigo 7.º
Função dos instrumentos internacionais

A lei aplicável a um contrato por força do presente instrumento pode ser interpretada, complementada e desenvolvida de acordo com os instrumentos enumerados no Artigo 4º, nº 3[209].

---

207 Cf. Regulamento Roma I, Art. 4, nº1, al. g); Projeto de Lei da República Democrática do Congo, Art. 3º, nº 1, al. f). As soluções alternativas que podem ser consideradas incluem leis modelo (Neels e Fredericks (n 1, 2018) pp. 352-354) e a aplicação da lei do país da prestação característica do contrato, tal como estabelecido no contrato (*ibidem*, p. 354-355).

208 Cf. Regulamento Roma I, Art. 4º, com algumas alterações substantivas e linguísticas.

209 Cf. Princípios da UNIDROIT, Preâmbulo, Par. 6; Convenção Interamericana sobre a Lei Aplicável aos Contratos

Artigo 8.º
Aceitação e validade substancial; escolha de lei em cláusulas contratuais gerais conflituantes (*battle of forms*)

1. A existência e a validade substancial do contrato, ou de alguma das suas disposições, são reguladas pela lei que lhes seria aplicável por força do presente instrumento se o contrato ou a disposição fossem válidos[210].
2. Todavia, a lei do país em que um contraente tem a sua residência habitual determina se o contraente deu o seu consentimento em relação ao contrato, ou a alguma das suas disposições, se, em circunstâncias particulares, não for razoável determinar os efeitos do seu comportamento nos termos da lei designada no nº 1[211].
3. Caso as partes tenham usado dois conjuntos de cláusulas contratuais gerais que designem leis diferentes, ou se uma lei é apenas designada por um dos conjuntos[212], entende-se não haver escolha expressa de lei[213].

Artigo 9.º
Validade formal

1. A escolha de lei não está sujeita a qualquer requisito de forma, salvo acordo das partes em contrário[214].
2. Sem prejuízo do nº 1, um contrato é formalmente válido se preencher os requisitos a este respeito de pelo menos um dos seguintes sistemas jurídicos:

Internacionais, Arts. 9º e 10º. V. Neels e Fredericks (n 1, 2018) p. 350.

210   Cf. Regulamento Roma I, Art. 10º, nº 1; Princípios da Haia, Art. 6º, nº 1, al. a).

211   Cf. Princípios da Haia, Art. 6º, nº 2; Regulamento Roma I, Art. 10º, nº 2.

212   O Art. 6º, nº 1, al. b) dos Princípios da Haia não prevê (expressamente) esta hipótese.

213   Cf. Princípios da Haia, Art. 6º, nº 1, al. b); Neels e Fredericks (n 1, 2018) p. 352 e bibliografia aí referida.

214   Cf. Princípios da Haia, Art. 5º.

(a) a lei do país da celebração do contrato, determinada de acordo com (i) a lei do foro, ou (ii) a lei aplicável ao contrato por força do presente instrumento;

(b) a lei aplicável ao contrato por força do presente instrumento[215];

(c) a lei do país em que qualquer uma das partes do contrato tem a sua residência habitual;

(d) a lei do país em que o agente de qualquer uma das partes do contrato tem a sua residência habitual[216];

(e) a lei do país em que as obrigações decorrentes do contrato devam ser executadas[217].

3. Como exceção ao nº 2, mas sem prejuízo do nº 1, a validade formal de uma disposição de um contrato que tem por objeto um direito real sobre um bem imóvel, ou o arrendamento de um bem imóvel, é regulada pela lei do país onde o imóvel se situa[218].

Artigo 10.º
Reenvio

A aplicação da lei de um país designada pelo presente instrumento implica a aplicação das normas jurídicas em vigor nesse país, com exclusão das suas normas de direito internacional privado, salvo acordo expresso das partes em contrário[219].

Artigo 11.º
Normas de aplicação imediata

1. As normas de aplicação imediata são normas jurídicas consideradas fundamentais por um país para a

---

215 Cf. Princípios da Haia, Art. 9º, nº 1, al. e) e nº 2.
216 Cf. Regulamento Roma I, Art. 11º.
217 Convenção Interamericana, Art. 13º.
218 Cf. Regulamento Roma I, Art. 11º, nº 5.
219 Cf. Princípios da Haia, Art. 8º; Regulamento Roma I, Art. 20º; Lei Modelo da UNCITRAL sobre Arbitragem Comercial Internacional, Art. 28º, nº1.

salvaguarda do interesse público (designadamente a sua organização política, social ou económica) ao ponto de exigir a sua aplicação em qualquer situação abrangida pelo seu âmbito de aplicação, independentemente da lei que de outro modo seria aplicável ao contrato por força do presente instrumento.

2. As normas de aplicação imediata da lei aplicável ao contrato por força do presente instrumento são, em princípio, aplicáveis.

3. Pode ser dada prevalência às normas de aplicação imediata:

    (a) da lei do foro;
    (b) da lei do país em que as obrigações decorrentes do contrato devam ser executadas (incluindo o país em que tem lugar o começo, continuação ou conclusão de tal execução).

4. Em circunstâncias excecionais, as normas de aplicação imediata de outro país podem ser aplicadas desde que a lei em questão tenha uma conexão manifestamente estreita com a situação concreta.

5. Para decidir se deve ser dada prevalência a qualquer uma das normas de aplicação imediata mencionadas nos n°s 3 ou 4, devem ser tidos em conta a sua natureza e o seu objeto, bem como as consequências da sua aplicação ou não aplicação[220].

Artigo 12.º
Ordem pública do foro

A aplicação de uma disposição da lei de um país designada pelo presente instrumento só pode ser afastada se essa aplicação for manifestamente incompatível com a ordem pública do foro[221].

---

220 Cf. Convenção de Roma sobre a Lei Aplicável às Obrigações Contratuais, Art. 7º; Regulamento Roma I, Art. 9º; Princípios da Haia, Art. 11º, n°s 1, 2 e 5.

221 Cf. Regulamento Roma I, Art. 21º; Princípios da Haia, Art. 11º, n°s 3 a 5.

Artigo 13.º
Âmbito da lei aplicável ao contrato

1. A lei aplicável a um contrato por força do presente instrumento regula todos os aspetos do contrato celebrado entre as partes, nomeadamente mas não só:

    (a) a interpretação[222];
    (b) os direitos e as obrigações decorrentes do contrato[223];
    (c) as diversas causas de extinção das obrigações, bem como a prescrição e a caducidade[224];
    (d) as consequências da invalidade formal ou substancial do contrato[225];
    (e) o ónus da prova e presunções legais[226];
    (f) as obrigações pré-contratuais[227].

2.

    (a) A lei aplicável ao contrato por força do presente instrumento regula o cumprimento[228] e as consequências do incumprimento total ou parcial das obrigações que decorrem do contrato, incluindo a avaliação do dano[229] na medida em que esta avaliação seja regulada pela lei[230].
    (b) Todavia, um tribunal ou tribunal arbitral pode recusar-se a conceder indemnizações nos termos da lei aplicável por força da alínea a) na medida em que

---

222 Cf. Princípios da Haia, Art. 9º, nº 1, al. a); Regulamento Roma I, Art. 12º, nº 1, a).
223 Cf. Princípios da Haia, Art. 9º, nº 1, al. b).
224 Cf. Princípios da Haia, Art. 9º, nº 1, al. d); Regulamento Roma I, Art. 12º, nº 1, d).
225 Cf. Princípios da Haia, Art. 9º, nº 1, al. e); Regulamento Roma I, Art. 12º, nº 1, e).
226 Cf. Princípios da Haia, Art. 9º, nº 1, al. f); Regulamento Roma I, Art. 18º, nº 1.
227 Cf. Princípios da Haia, Art. 9º, nº 1, al. g).
228 Cf. Princípios da Haia, Art. 9º, nº 1, al. c); Regulamento Roma I, Art. 12º, nº 1, b).
229 Cf. Princípios da Haia, Art. 9º, nº 1, al. c); Regulamento Roma I, Art. 12º, nº 1, c).
230 Cf. Regulamento Roma I, Art. 12º, nº 1, c).

os danos excedam a compensação pela perda (danos exemplares ou punitivos)[231].

(c) Não obstante, um tribunal ou tribunal arbitral deve ter em conta se e em que medida a indemnização de carácter exemplar ou punitivo nos termos da lei aplicável ao contrato serve para cobrir as custas e despesas relacionadas com o processo[232].

(d) Quanto aos modos de cumprimento e às medidas que o credor deve tomar no caso de cumprimento defeituoso, deve atender-se à lei do país do lugar acordado para o cumprimento[233].

Artigo 14.º
Compensação

A compensação é regulada pela lei aplicável ao crédito contra o qual se invoca a compensação, salvo acordo das partes em contrário[234].

Artigo 15.º
Residência habitual

1. Para efeitos do presente instrumento, a residência habitual de sociedades e outras entidades dotadas ou não de personalidade jurídica é o local onde se situa a sua administração central[235].

---

231 V. Regulamento Roma II, considerando nº 32; cf. Convenção da Haia sobre os Acordos de Eleição do Foro, Art. 11º, nº 1; Convenção da Haia sobre o Reconhecimento e a Execução de Sentenças Estrangeiras em Matéria Civil ou Comercial, Art. 10º, nº 1.

232 Cf. Convenção da Haia sobre os Acordos de Eleição do Foro, Art. 11º, nº 2; Convenção da Haia sobre o Reconhecimento e a Execução de Sentenças Estrangeiras em Matéria Civil ou Comercial, Art. 10º, nº 2.

233 Cf. Regulamento Roma I, Art. 12º, nº 2.

234 Cf. Regulamento Roma I, Art. 17º.

235 Cf. Regulamento Roma I, Art. 19º, nº 1.

2. A residência habitual de uma pessoa singular, no exercício da sua atividade profissional, situa-se no país do seu estabelecimento principal[236].

3. Caso o contrato seja celebrado no âmbito da exploração de uma sucursal, agência ou qualquer outro estabelecimento, ou se, nos termos do contrato, o cumprimento das obrigações dele decorrentes é da responsabilidade de tal sucursal, agência ou estabelecimento, considera-se que a residência habitual corresponde ao país onde se situa a sucursal, agência ou outro estabelecimento[237].

4. Para determinar a residência habitual, o momento relevante é a data da celebração do contrato[238].

Artigo 16.º
Interpretação e aplicação uniforme

Na interpretação do presente instrumento devem ser tidos em consideração o seu caráter regional e relevância internacional e a necessidade de promover a sua aplicação uniforme[239].

Artigo 17.º
Entrada em vigor e aplicação no tempo

O presente instrumento foi adotado pele União Africana em *[data]* e é aplicável aos contratos celebrados a partir de *[data]*. Em litígios relativos a contratos celebrados antes desta data,

---

236 Cf. Regulamento Roma I, Art. 19º, nº 1; Fredericks (n 35) p. 248.

237 Cf. Regulamento Roma I, Art. 19º, nº 2; Princípios da Haia, Art. 12º.

238 Cf. Regulamento Roma I, Art. 19º, nº 3.

239 Cf. Convenção das Nações Unidas sobre Contratos para Venda Internacional de Mercadorias, Art. 7º, nº 1; Convenção Interamericana, Art. 4º; Convenção da Haia sobre os Acordos de Eleição do Foro, Art. 23º; Convenção da Haia sobre o Reconhecimento e a Execução de Sentenças Estrangeiras em Matéria Civil ou Comercial, Art. 20º.

o tribunal ou tribunal arbitral pode ter em consideração as disposições do presente instrumento[240].

58

---

240   Em relação à segunda frase v. Projeto de Lei da República Democrática do Congo, Art. 24º (segunda frase).

Bibliography in Respect of the African Principles

Faadhil **Adams** *Choice of Non-State Law in International Commercial Contracts* (doctoral thesis, University of Johannesburg, 2023)

Garth J **Bouwers** *Tacit Choice of Law in International Commercial Contracts – A Global Comparative Study* (Schulthess, 2021)

Garth J **Bouwers** "Tacit choice of law in international commercial contracts. An analysis of future instruments of developmental organisations" 2023 *Potchefstroom Electronic Law Journal* (to be published)

Eesa A **Fredericks** *Contractual Capacity in Private International Law* (Meijers Research Institute, University of Leiden, 2016)

Sai Ramani **Garimella** and Mukesh **Rawat** "Daniel Girsberger *et al* (eds) *Choice of Law in International Commercial Contracts: Global Perspectives on the Hague Principles*" 2021 *Netherlands International Law Review* 501

Peter **Mankowski** "Daniel Girsberger *et al* (eds) *Choice of Law in International Commercial Contracts: Global Perspectives on the Hague Principles*" 2022 *Internationales Handelsrecht* 43

Justin **Monsenepwo** "*Quo vadis,* OHADA private international law?" 2021 *Uniform Law Review/Revue de droit uniforme* 345

Justin **Monsenepwo** "L'Avant-projet de Loi sur la loi applicable aux obligations contractuelles en droit international privé congolais" in T K Bala *et al Adoption des mineurs et migrations en droit interne, international et comparé* Tome II *Mélanges en l'honneur du Professeur Paolo Morozzo della Rocca* (Editions Universitaires Européennes, Paris, 2021) 604

Annelies **Nachtergaele** "Harmonization of private international law in the Southern African Development Community" 2014/2015 *Yearbook of Private International Law* 365

Jan L **Neels** "The African Principles on the Law Applicable to International Commercial Contracts – a first drafting experiment" 2020 *Uniform Law Review/Revue de droit uniforme* 426

Jan L **Neels** "Characterisation and liberative prescription (the limitation of actions) in private international law – Canadian doctrine in the Eswatini courts (the phenomenon of dual cumulation)" 2021 *Journal of Private International Law* 361

Jan L **Neels** "International commercial law emerging in Africa" 2022 *Potchefstroom Electronic Law Journal* (Special Edition: *Festschrift Charl Hugo*) DOI http://dx.doi.org/10.17159/1727-3781/2022/v25i0a14381

Jan L **Neels** "The Southern African Development Community and the African Principles on the Law Applicable to International Commercial Contracts" in Moses Retselisitsoe **Phooko**, Lloyd Tonderai **Chigowe** and Hoolo **'Nyane** (eds) *The Development and Application of SADC Community Law in Member States* (Juta, 2023) ch 8 (forthcoming)

Jan L **Neels** "Law of obligations: South Africa" in Stellina **Jolly** and Saloni **Khanderia** (eds) *Private International Law in BRICS: Convergence, Divergence and Reciprocal Lessons* (Hart/Bloomsbury, 2024) (forthcoming) [the chapter contains a comparison of positive South African private international law of contract and the African Principles on the Law Applicable to International Commercial Contracts]

Jan L **Neels** and Eesa A **Fredericks** "An introduction to the African Principles of Commercial Private International Law" 2018 *Stellenbosch Law Review* 34

Jan L **Neels** and Eesa A **Fredericks** "The African Principles of Commercial Private International Law and the Hague Principles" in Daniel **Girsberger**, Thomas **Kadner Graziano** and Jan L **Neels** (gen eds) *Choice of Law in International Commercial Contracts. Global Perspectives on the Hague Principles* (Oxford University Press, 2021) 239

Jan L **Neels** and Eesa A **Fredericks** "Covid-19 regulations as overriding mandatory provisions in private international law

– a comparison of regional, supranational and international instruments with the proposed African Principles on the Law Applicable to International Commercial Contracts" in Murdoch Watney (ed) *The Impact of COVID-19 on the Future of Law and Related Disciplines* (University of Johannesburg Press, 2022) 1

Jan L **Neels**, Eesa A **Fredericks** and Solomon **Okorley** "UNIDROIT and Africa – UNIDROIT Principles and African Principles" in Ben **Köhler**, Rishi **Gulati** and Thomas **John** (eds) *The Elgar Companion to UNIDROIT* (Edward Elgar, 2024) ch 3 (forthcoming)

Chukwuma Samuel Adesina **Okoli** "International commercial litigation in English-speaking Africa: a critical review" 2020 *Journal of Private International Law* 189

Chukwuma Samuel Adesina **Okoli** "The significance of a forum selection agreement as an indicator of the implied choice of law in international contracts: a global comparative perspective" 2023 *Uniform Law Review/Revue de droit uniforme* https://doi.org/10.1093/ulr/unad016

Chukwuma Samuel Adesina **Okoli** and Richard Frimpong **Oppong** "Some critical responses to the Draft African Principles on the Law Applicable to International Commercial Contracts" (forthcoming)

Chukwuma Samuel Adesina **Okoli** and Abubakri **Yekini** "Implied jurisdiction agreements: a global comparative perspective" (forthcoming, *Journal of Private International Law*)

Richard Frimpong **Oppong** *Legal Aspects of Economic Integration in Africa* (Cambridge University Press, 2011)

Richard Frimpong **Oppong** *Private International Law in Commonwealth Africa* (Cambridge University Press, 2013)

Priskila **Penasthika** *Unravelling Choice of Law in International Commercial Contracts. Indonesia as an Illustrative Case Study* (Eleven, 2022)

Marlene M **Wethmar-Lemmer** "The three pillars of regulating international sales contracts on the African continent" (inaugural lecture, 19 October 2023, University of South Africa) (forthcoming)

The Author

Prof Jan L Neels is Distinguished Professor of Private International Law / International Commercial Law, specialising in Commercial Private International Law, director of the Research Centre for Private International Law in Emerging Countries and course-coordinator of the flagship LLM programme in International Commercial Law at the University of Johannesburg. He studied at the Rand Afrikaans University (BCom, LLB and LLM degrees *cum laude*) and was awarded the doctoral degree from the University of Leiden (the doctrine of the abuse of rights). He has more than 70 articles and chapters in his name, published in Germany, Italy, the Netherlands, Paraguay, South Africa, Switzerland, Türkiye and the United Kingdom. He was cited more than ten times by the High Courts in South Africa, including five citations by the Supreme Court of Appeal. Prof Neels delivered papers at the Hague Academy of International Law, the Max Planck Institute for Foreign and International Private Law and the Department of International Relations and Cooperation (DIRCO). He also read papers at various foreign universities, including the universities of Amsterdam, Antwerp, British Columbia (Centre for Asian Legal Studies), Cambridge, Coimbra, Innsbruck, Leiden, Lucerne, Namibia, Saarland, Tilburg and Zaragoza, as well as universities in France (Aix-en-Provence), India (South Asian University in Delhi) and Türkiye (Özyeğin and Yeditepe, both in Istanbul). Prof Neels submitted reports to DIRCO, the European Commission (revision of the Rome Convention on the Law Applicable to Contractual Obligations), the Hague Conference on Private International Law (revision of the preliminary draft Uniform Law on the Law of Obligations (section conflict of laws), *Organisation pour l'harmonisation en Afrique du droit des affaires*), the Inter-American Juridical Committee of the Organization of American States (revision of the Mexico City Convention), the International Academy of Comparative Law, the International Association of Procedural Law and the South African Law Reform Commission. Prof Neels was a member of the Working Group and Special Commission (including its Drafting Committee) formulating the Hague Principles on Choice of Law in International Commercial Contracts (2015) under the auspices of the Hague Conference on Private International Law. Prof Neels was a member of the Governing Council of UNIDROIT for the period 2014–2018. He is currently an honorary member of this body, as well as a member of the Academy of Science of South Africa. He was one of the general editors of Girsberger, Kadner Graziano and Neels *Choice of Law in International Commercial Contracts. Global Perspectives on the Hague Principles* (OUP, 2021). Prof Neels recently published a first draft of the African Principles on the Law Applicable to International Commercial Contracts.